Broken For The Promise

by
Chasity Strawder

Dedication

To my Lord and Savior, Jesus Christ, who carried me when I was too weak to walk, held me in His warm embrace, and covered me with His amazing grace.

To my parents, Willie and Peggy Washington, for raising me in the admonition of the Lord.

To my loving husband, Terrence, for his unending love and support through the darkest days of my life.

To my sons, Donovan and Joshua, who have my heart eternally.

And to my friends, family, and associates for your faithful support.

Introduction

I met my husband, Terrence while I was an elementary school teacher in Ann Arbor, Michigan. He worked part time at a gas station around the corner from the school. I stopped there in the mornings for coffee, and soon we became acquainted with each other. I was a year shy of turning thirty years old. We dated for about a year before Terrence finally proposed. After our marriage, four years later, I discovered that I was pregnant. Things were going well until I started bleeding one day. This resulted in a visit to the emergency room where we were told that the heartbeat could not be detected. My hormonal levels continued to drop, and I eventually miscarried.

I soon became pregnant again a few weeks later with our youngest son Joshua. It was indeed the most difficult journey of my human experience due to a diagnosis of gastro paresis. I had no understanding as to why or how I acquired this deadly disease, but I was in for the fight of my life. I spent the duration of the pregnancy in the emergency room, or being admitted as a patient into the hospital. No medication that was prescribed lessened the symptoms, and there were no words that could ease the pain.

Table of Contents

Chapter 1

Trusting God

Trusting God is a decision that is easier said than done. It goes beyond regular church attendance, religious jargon, or biblical knowledge. It is birthed out of a true relationship with Jesus Christ. In this walk with Him, there is a commitment to be faithful to His ways and commands no matter how dark the path may be at a given time. We can be the most relaxed about trusting God when everything is peaceful and prosperous, but what about those times when things are stormy and unfavorable? God still has a plan for our lives even when we are simply walking through, and don't know where we will end up or how to get there.

Jeremiah 29:11 declares, "For I know the

thoughts I think toward you, saith the Lord, thoughts of peace, and not of evil, to give you an expected end." We can trust in God, for His ways are always rooted in His unfailing love for us, and we can always count on everything working out for our good in the end. When the heat of trials has been turned up and the pains of life seem overwhelming, it is very easy to believe that God is against us and not for us. It is always the intention of the adversary to use negative circumstances to forge a wall between us and our Redeemer.

Even with everything that Job had lost and the constant reminder to curse his God, he still displayed his faith in God when he said, "For I know that my redeemer liveth, and that he shall stand at the latter day upon the earth" (Job 19:25). Job clearly must have reached a breaking point in his suffering, but he paused to reflect on the presence of God in the midst of it all. Although he was at the brink of dying and had been abandoned by his friends, Job prayed for his friends and what he had lost was restored double to him.

In 2 Corinthians 12, Paul had a "thorn" that he asked God to remove several times to no avail. God's only response to him was given in verse 9: *And he said unto me, my grace is sufficient for thee: for my strength is made perfect in weakness. Most gladly will I rather glory in my infirmities that the power of Christ may rest upon me.* Paul realized that he was walking in a greater strength and power beyond his own by submitting his will to the will of God for his life. Joy was the response to the magnitude of his troubles. The joy is not "for" the difficulties, but "for" the presence of God that promises to abide with us no matter what may come or go.

The question remains: Will we allow these trials and tribulations to truly separate us from God? John 16:33 reads, "In the world you shall

3

have tribulation: but be of good cheer; I have overcome the world." The keyword is "overcome", and it is not completely up to God to decide that outcome for us. We also determine our outcomes through our perseverance and faith in His promises. Romans 8:37-39 states, "Nay, in all these things we are more than conquerors through him that loved us. For I am persuaded, that neither death, nor life, nor angels, nor principalities, nor powers or nor things present, nor things to come. Nor height, nor depth, nor any other creature shall be able to separate us from the love of God, which is in Christ Jesus our Lord."

Sometimes it is safe to say that if we don't sense the presence of God, especially during times of trials, it may be because we have moved away from God. He has promised to never leave nor forsake us. A firm trust in God does not occur overnight, but in adequate fellowship with Him through reading His word and prayer. We can hold on to Him as he holds on to us.

In the pages that follow, you will accompany me on a dark journey through a difficult period in my life. My faith in God was tested on a level that I had never experienced before in my years as a Christian. I had been brought up in a Bible-believing home. My life had been dedicated to serving God through faithful church attendance and through a personal relationship with Him; nevertheless, nothing could have prepared me for the pain ahead of me.

My journey was extremely difficult because the pain went on for a long time with very little relief or real answers. I did have moments of mental and emotional breakdowns, also of extreme impatience. However, my connection to God grew stronger because I knew that He was the only one who could help me get through this time. I couldn't always formulate prayers to Him, so I would cry for hours on end while clasping my hands very tightly. Many people prayed for me throughout my ordeal. It was very frustrating that the pain of it wasn't removed immediately, but the grace to endure it would come on a daily basis. My determination to be strong and to get to the other side of the pain made me a survivor and a conqueror. I am sitting here writing this as a testimony that anything is possible with God. Hang on with me for the ride of your life!

Chapter 2

In the Beginning

I always considered myself a pretty solid
Christian, grounded in God while holding firmly
to my beliefs. I gave my life to Christ at the age
of nine years old, and I was raised in a
Christian home where church attendance and
biblical principles were instilled in me. I've
always loved God, taking His words and
presence in my life very seriously. I knew by
the personal encounters that I had as a child
that He was very real to me. Truthfully, I don't
remember ever truly existing without Him. Of
course, life had its share of ups and downs,
turmoil and disappointments, acceptances and
rejections, but the foundation of my faith had
always gotten me up and going again. Little did
I know that the year 2010 would test all that I

professed to be throughout my life. It was indeed the darkest period of my existence.

It all started with a miscarriage in early 2010, about six weeks into the pregnancy of my first child with my husband, Terrence. There we were surprised, but overjoyed at the news of a coming baby, only to be devastated from a sonogram that showed no signs of a heartbeat. We held onto our faith until the end, believing that my hormone levels would regulate, and the pregnancy would proceed as planned. To our surprise, I continued to bleed, and before we knew it, the end had come. I was pretty numb throughout that period, not really knowing how to grieve or sort out my feelings. As far as I had known, I had always been healthy. My first pregnancy had been complication-free, and I had delivered my son, Donovan, at full term. I just didn't understand why this had happened. I released a lot of my emotions through worship. I didn't know how I would communicate to God how hurt and disappointed I was. My husband was given godly instructions to comfort me, and to allow me to vent as needed. I only found myself really feeling the pain during worship or if someone pointed out to me that I looked sad or lost.

I thought the bleeding would never stop. It was like a lingering reminder that was desperately hanging on to ruin my life. After three or four weeks, I was starting to feel normal again. Sex is truly the greatest act of comfort between a man and a woman after such an unfortunate event, more than some would probably care to admit. I remember that night like it was yesterday. Being in Terrence's arms was simply magical. Those memories turned to horror when I found myself being taken to the emergency room for persistent nausea and

vomiting. It started out like a choking
sensation, and then I heaved until I had been
spent. After numerous questions and tests, the
words "You are pregnant" were uttered to
Terrence and I. I was five weeks along to be
exact. We were expecting again just a few
weeks shy of suffering a miscarriage. These
very unpleasant symptoms appeared to be the
great nightmare of the first trimester of the
pregnancy. Yuck! I was in for a long ride
indeed. I was released to go home with a
referral to see an obstetrician right away.
To our utter dismay, the nausea and vomiting
did not go away; it only grew worse. I didn't
believe it was just "morning sickness". The pain
I was experiencing went way beyond what
morning sickness felt like on any given day. I
was referred to a gastroenterologist for further
testing. I underwent an endoscopy of my
esophagus and stomach at about eight weeks
pregnant. The risks involved were greater

because I was still very delicate and not quite out of my first trimester. I was very scared, but agreed to the procedure because desperation had started setting in at that point. The trips to the emergency room were becoming more frequent because of the severe dehydration. There were no real answers following the endoscopy. The concerns were that the hormonal changes were beating up my gut severely and slowing down digestion. While staying overnight in the observation unit of a hospital, I was very calmly advised by one of the attending physicians that I could consider the option to abort the fetus. He said that I was still within the time perimeters to "safely" abort my child. He then told me that it was my body and my decision. I was devastated. Another doctor thought I was simply depressed about the news of being pregnant again so soon. This was all very far from the truth. Something was wrong with me. I just couldn't articulate what it was or how it could be fixed. Every antacid known to mankind was suggested to provide some sort of relief, but they didn't work. Terrence and I found ourselves so frustrated that we sought out another gastrointestinal doctor. We found a new gastrointestinal doctor, and he suspected that the issue was "gastro paresis" in the pregnancy. Of course, we didn't understand how I could have gastro paresis considering I did not have a history of diabetes. The new diagnosis was strange and scary. I had so much further to go in my pregnancy, yet I felt that I was not going to get through another day. The weakness, pain, nausea, and vomiting was becoming unbearable. I was prescribed a regiment of Protonix, and in between my prescription, the doctor recommended that I take over-the-counter antacids to help me keep my food down. The Gastroenterologist also tested some other drugs out on me that simply didn't work. Lying in bed was becoming the norm, and when things got too bad, I went to the emergency room where I had to explain everything all over again and get re-hydrated.

On one particular occasion, I'd spent a couple of days in the hospital and several more days in the emergency room. I was not gaining weight, so I was being monitored by a calorie counter. My Obstetrician would annoy me by repeatedly telling me to get down what I could. The hardest part was the lack of real concern with the doctors and specialists. No one really knew how to treat my condition, and the emotional pain was beyond their human comprehension. Besides my ongoing health issue, the medical bills (mostly co-pays) and other expenses were mounting. Terrence was working full-time as a manager in a cancer research lab, but I couldn't help him with our bills. I was just too sick.

Chapter 3

Moving Out

We eventually got behind on our rent and had to make a decision about our living arrangements. We couldn't pay all of the money that was owed, so we prepared to move out of our residence. We put our large furniture items in storage and moved into a one-room motel with the rest of our stuff. The room was small but had two beds, a small desk with a lamp, a microwave, and a refrigerator. There was a recliner in the corner of the room. The motel was clean and the staff there was very nice. In the morning, a small continental breakfast was offered. Coffee and tea were set up in the lobby for self-serve all day long. Terrence was still working so I found myself alone during the day trying to battle with what was going on in my body and mind. Terrence would take off work whenever he could to take me to the emergency room, and sometimes, he would stay with me to give me that extra comfort I needed. My Gastroenterologist suggested that I try to sleep sitting up in the recliner to minimize the effects of the acid that was causing most of the vomiting. Even that option didn't work. I was getting up to vomit during the night, but the worst of it was in the morning after lying flat all night. The hormones were causing my sphincter muscle to remain open so that everything that I ingested never stayed in my body. Anything I ate came back up with force. I would fall asleep on the floor of the bathroom after puking my guts up. Sometimes I wouldn't make it to the toilet so the sink was the next best thing. I vomited all over myself while in bed sometimes. Terrence would help me to the bathroom, but by the time I had gotten back in bed, the vomiting would have started all over again.

I knew that I was dying. I was feeling my body shut down more and more as the days went by. My body was not retaining the nutrients I needed to keep me going. I was given a referral for a high risk pregnancy doctor. My doctor visits were multiplying with no answers in sight. The next option was to have me fitted for a feeding tube, with a nurse to come and monitor my health a couple of days a week. There was no guarantee that it would even work. The risk of infection would be greater with a line running through my body. We decided against it and the emergency room visits continued as needed. Eating & drinking anything was a gamble because we didn't know if it would stay down or not. Most of the times, the food did not stay down.

I found that the baby moved the least when I was dehydrated. The concern was for my health the most because the baby was coming along in development. The measurements were normal, and the baby's position was always head down. I remember grabbing Terrence's hand when I was about 16 weeks along and begging him to let me "get rid of it." I was desperate to relieve myself of the constant pain and turmoil. With tears in his eyes, he told me that we were going to get through it together. I cried my eyes out that night until sleep overtook me. The constant vomiting and dehydration left me feeling weak and in a lot of pain. I wasn't gaining enough weight to balance the weight of the baby. My back, legs, and abdomen were the most painful areas. Opening and closing my legs were followed by deep grimaces of pain. Marital intimacy was out of the question. Pelvic exams at my appointments were virtually impossible. Monitoring of the baby was done mostly by ultrasounds. The baby's heartbeat was steady and strong.

Chapter 4

Finding Another Way

I found myself turning to alternative medicine as a way to relieve my symptoms. I talked to a friend of mine who was trained in herbal and homeopathic medicines. I tried a few at first, but was never successfully relieved of anything. I was then given a referral to an acupuncturist. I started seeing her about twice a week. It was a bit of a drive from where the motel was, but at that point, the distance didn't really matter. Our medical insurance didn't cover acupuncture, but the doctor didn't charge me because of how sorry she felt for me. I believe that she was an angel sent from God. She wiped away my tears and worked on me with all of her might when things were really bad. Our conversations helped me to take my mind off things a little and think about the growing baby inside of me. By that time, we knew that we were having a boy. I was excited because I had asked God for a boy who looked like his dad. My oldest son, Donovan, looks more like me.

I shared custody of Donovan with his dad. Donovan came to visit us at the motel. It was hard to hide my illness from him because we were living in very cramped conditions. I tried to restrict my visits to the emergency room to the days when he was not with us. I knew that he was worried about me because I would catch him looking at me with watery eyes. I couldn't always hide the vomiting from him, but I tried to show him that I was strong in spite of it all. I continued to get up and help him get ready for school, and I would drive him to school whenever I was able to. I was also serving as the president of the parent board at

Donovan's school. The principal and other members of the staff knew about my delicate condition and offered many soothing words of encouragement. I knew that they were offering up prayers on my behalf. I tried to remain mobile as much as possible because being mobile allowed me to be around people. It was also weird to have people stare at me or wonder how I was pregnant. After all, I hadn't gained any weight; instead, I was losing weight. My little round stomach was the biggest thing on my body. I had lost most of my body fat and my muscles had weakened tremendously. I wore baggy clothes to cover my frail body. Our motel was located across the parking lot from a McDonald's. I would often find myself walking to McDonald's to grab a small fry and a large orange drink. The salt from the fries felt refreshing to my body. It was in those moments that life felt somewhat normal, even if only temporarily.

We still had money woes staring us in the face. The motel manager would give us extensions to pay our rent. We still had to monitor our spending because we had no way to cook food. God still made provision for us, and the money that we had stretched enough to meet our needs. There was not a lot of extra, but we made things work. Pizza and sandwiches were consumed often, we kept drinks in our fridge, and microwaveable foods were eaten in moderation. Most of the time, Terrence and I were alone so we were able to stretch our food as well. Food Network, Travel Channel, and Facebook were my distractions on the really bad days. I prayed a lot, mostly crying out to God for the removal of my pain. There were days when I vomited and prayed, prayed and vomited. I kept a trash can nearby. I didn't understand why my illness didn't go completely away, but it didn't stop me from reaching out to God through my prayers and tears. Sometimes

24

I couldn't form the prayers, but a song would come to mind as a means of comfort. The vomiting didn't go away, but the strength to endure it for another day would come. The funny thing was that I actually felt closer to God during this horrific time in my life than I'd ever felt before. I just didn't understand why this was happening and how it would be fixed. Our church attendance had dwindled to a minimum. Our church was located in Toledo, Ohio, and I couldn't sit through a service or endure the long drive back to the motel. The total travel time was well over an hour and a half. However, it was actually during one of the rides to church that God spoke to me about naming our son Joshua. There was an excitement that rose up inside of me when I heard His clear, audible voice. It was also pretty amazing that the sermon was taken from the book of Joshua that Sunday. I turned and smiled at Terrence because I knew what I'd heard was from God.

We decided to give our son the middle name Owen, because it is part of my husband's middle name. What we didn't know at the time was that our situation was getting ready to take another weird twist on the road of getting our baby safely delivered.

Chapter 5

A New Doctor

There was a time when I had switched to a different Obstetrician, and he was Asian. The new doctor did his job, but didn't offer a lot of understanding or compassion to me. The focus was more on trying new things to get Joshua safely delivered. I was almost through my eighth month of pregnancy, and the misery was beyond what words could express. My Obstetrician's concern was for the development of Joshua's lungs. If his lungs were underdeveloped, we'd be in for a very long hospital stay with a lot of possible complications. Having a premature baby would be an added stress for us considering all we had been through already. Nevertheless, the only way for us to know for sure if the baby would be born prematurely was to have an amniocentesis. The procedure would have to be done at the hospital in a regular labor and delivery room, just in case I started to have contractions. A fetal heart monitor would be attached to me the entire time to track the baby's heart rate.

We were finally scheduled to come in for the amniocentesis. The thought of a long needle being inserted inside my body without any kind of numbing medication horrified me. I was told that the needle normally used for the numbing medication was longer and thicker than the needle to draw the fluid. For this reason, it was not used for this procedure. The doctor said it would prolong the procedure by causing more pain.

When we arrived in the room, I got changed into my hospital gown and was hooked up to a fetal heart monitor. I was also prepped to get an intravenous needle because I was still vomiting, plus I was dehydrated. As usual, it was difficult for the doctor to insert the IV because my veins had been damaged from all of the emergency room visits and hospital stays. There had been times when the nurses or techs had to use a machine to help locate an "edible" vein. Finally, the IV was in, and I was waiting on the doctor to come in to begin the procedure. I was in so much pain, I thought I was going to crush Terrence's hand. I was also gritting my teeth severely as the long needle went into my body to draw the fluid from my amniotic sack. I had to endure a few minutes of agony, but those minutes felt like hours. I had to stay hooked on the fetal heart monitor for at least an hour after the procedure to ensure I didn't go into active labor. There were a few contractions, but they were so mild that I couldn't feel anything. Before I knew it, the time had come to get dressed and leave. It would be another ten days before we knew the results of the test. I was told that I would be sore at the injection site for a few days, but sore was an understatement. It was very painful. I put a warm towel on myself to get a little bit of relief.

Finally, we received the call that we had been waiting for. The amniocentesis had revealed that the baby's lungs were not mature, so delivery would be too dangerous at that point. I was devastated and I cried repeatedly. I was told that delivering my baby would probably put an end to all of the sickness I'd been enduring. My hormones would be normal, and all would be well again. I could not believe that I had to wait another four weeks to deliver my baby. I was devastated. I remember so clearly that Terrence and I sat in the car for a little while to pray. I think our tears were the same because of the heaviness of our hearts. We held hands and shared our pain with God. He had been with us through all of this, and somehow we were going to get through it. The thought of four more weeks seemed like an eternity to me, and I continued to see the acupuncturist at least twice a week. Sometimes she left some special kind of needles in my skin to help decrease the vomiting. They were covered up with clear tape. Some were placed on the palms of my hands, my lower abdomen, my back, and on the sides of my neck. I tried to cover them with my clothes as much as possible. Sometimes I couldn't hide them, and I received a lot of stares from people. However, the awkward stares didn't matter because I was still alive.

Chapter 6

Going Under

I was eager to get my pregnancy over and done with. My doctor was willing to do another amniocentesis. At that time, I was at the beginning of my ninth month, and I had about three more weeks to go. The amniocentesis was scheduled once again at the hospital, and when we arrived, I was prepped for the procedure. The doctor came in, and I grabbed Terrence's hand. Everything became quite fuzzy after that. I just remember the doctor withdrawing the needle, and I felt myself get really dizzy. What happened after that moment was from the account of my husband. I was now unconscious and could not respond to anyone speaking to me. My husband told me that a button was pushed inside of the room and then a lot of the hospital's staff came rushing in. He was escorted out of the room while they tried to get me to "come to." I ended up staying in the hospital until very late that night. I am not sure how long I was worked on, but things got really critical and scary for a while. I was discharged and my husband took me to a restaurant nearby. He told me what had happened, but I didn't remember any of it. He had to stop talking because he began to cry. To this day, it is very hard for him to talk about it, so I just don't bring it up. Even though it goes unsaid, we are aware of the fact that he could have lost me and Joshua for good. The doctor could not tell us why things happened the way they did. To make matters worse, the results came back confirming that the baby's lungs were still not mature enough for delivery. The only thing I could do was to wait to deliver my son at the beginning of my thirty-sixth week of pregnancy. By that time, the baby would be considered full-term without any major risks for complications.

Terrence and I started to realize that we had done very little to plan for the arrival of our baby because we'd been so focused on my illness. We put together a list of baby stuff that we needed and started hitting the stores. I rode around in the grocery scooters because I was too weak to walk. We picked up the basics and also purchased a car seat. Reality had begun to set in that I would soon be a mother again. Of course, the downside to it all was that we were still living in a motel; nevertheless, we were looking for another place to live. I was confident that God would provide at the right time. I was also still fighting through the nausea and vomiting. My doctor told me that I should count on having a vaginal birth. My body was too weak to deliver via Caesarian section. I didn't know how I was going to handle the contractions and push out a baby in my condition. I was really worried at this point, so I planned on getting an epidural to get me through the rough part. I talked to the acupuncturist about it, and her reassurance was comforting.

My induction was scheduled for the eve of Thanksgiving. I vomited that morning, but there was no time to focus on it because I had to prepare to be admitted to the hospital to have my baby. We arrived at about seven o'clock that evening. I went to the registration desk to pick up my room assignment and off to the elevator we went. I just wanted to get the pregnancy over with. We arrived at my room and I changed into my hospital gown. The nurse came in to put me on the monitor and to start the drip for the induction of my labor. After that, things began to progress very quickly. Within one hour, I was in active labor and begging for an epidural. My water had already broken. I was gripping Terrence's hand and the bed rails for dear life. The Anesthesiologist came in and started setting things up, and my memory of him is how mean he was. I was moaning in pain and he was more worried about getting me to stop moving than he was about my pain. My epidural was finally in place, but it didn't work. I didn't feel even one moment of relief. Terrence buzzed the nurse and told her the horrible news, and the Anesthesiologist was paged again. The nurse checked my progress, and I was fully dilated. The head was descending quickly. I had no choice but to start pushing. The pain was excruciating. There was no time for more pain medicine or a doctor. The nurse took her place at the head of the bed. I just remember being told to push really hard because Joshua's heart rate was decelerating. If he didn't come out within the next minute or so, a vacuum would be used. I gave it my best, and I felt him slide out. Terrence told me later that as Joshua came out my eyes started to roll back in my head. That moment was crucial for my well-being, just as it was for Joshua's. It was finally over.

Chapter 7

Joshua's Arrival

Just as the nurse was cleaning Joshua up, my
Obstetrician arrived. As quickly as the labor
had progressed along, with the few hard
pushes, it was over with. I didn't really tear at
all. I heard the doctor say that I only needed
one stitch. I was a mommy once again. Joshua
Owen Strawder weighed in at seven pounds
and eight ounces, and he was beautiful. They
finally handed him to me, and he started to
breast feed almost immediately. He stayed on
my breast for close to an hour.

The amazing part about the delivery was that
as hard as the pains were hitting me, I didn't
vomit one time. God had given me some well
needed relief. Joshua was circumcised the

next day, which was Thanksgiving Day. I was discharged to go home that evening. It was snowing pretty steadily. We stopped off at my brother-in-law's house to surprise his family and to grab some dinner. We left soon after to start the drive back to the motel. It wasn't a palace, but it was home for now.

Joshua had lost some weight in the hospital, so he was a little over six pounds. He seemed so tiny to me, but he was healthy. His appetite became demanding pretty quickly. I continued to breastfeed, and I used formula as a supplement. Terrence had been given time off from work, so we settled into the routine of being new parents. It was very hard to have a newborn in a motel; we didn't get a lot of sleep or relaxation. I was very sore from the delivery, so moving around was very difficult. We managed the best way we could and gave each other breaks as needed. To our dismay, I wasn't recovering from the gastro paresis as quickly as the doctors had said that I would. I was still having bouts of vomiting even after Joshua was born. I was feeling deceived and at my wits end, but hearing the coos of my baby and holding his warm body next to mine gave me hope. Somehow this nightmare that terrorized me for nine months was going to end soon, and I would be normal again.

Two weeks after having Joshua, I was seen by another gastrointestinal doctor, but he still could not explain why I wasn't better yet. I was scheduled for another endoscopy immediately. The doctor wanted to take another look at my esophagus, stomach, and intestines. The last thing I had to drink before midnight was some water. After that, I wasn't allowed to have anything. Terrence stayed in the waiting room with our precious Joshua while I went into the procedure room. After everything was over, the doctor told us that the water from the night before was still in my stomach. This indicated that my digestive system was extremely slow. This meant I still had gastro paresis. I was prescribed some medications but told that I wouldn't be able to continue breastfeeding. This was turning into a waiting game for my hormones to completely go back to normal. At that point, it had only been two weeks since Joshua's birth. I was scheduled to be seen by the gastrointestinal doctor after my first initial visit back to the Obstetrician for my six week checkup. Hearing that I still had gastro paresis was not the news that we were hoping for.

Joshua was doing really well. He was gaining weight and hadn't shown any signs of distress or trouble from everything that I had gone through. He was doing just fine. Needless to say, I wasn't. I was focused on being a good mother to my baby and getting well. My six week checkup revealed that I was healing nicely from the delivery. There were no other complications to report. My Obstetrician released me into the care of my primary care and gastrointestinal doctors.

Chapter 8

When It Rains, It Pours

About a month after Joshua was born, the engine in our car went completely out. It was too costly to fix so we sold the car to a junkyard. The payoff wasn't much and suddenly we were without a vehicle. This was another unexpected blow, but there wasn't much that could be done at that point. A friend of ours who lived nearby took us around to doctors' appointments and grocery shopping as needed. It was very difficult because we were stuck at the hotel without the freedom to get out and do things on our own. Renting a car was too expensive, and we were not in the position to finance another vehicle. The heaviness and discouragement from our situation was really starting to weigh on me.

Terrence and I prayed every day, but there
didn't seem to be an ending to what we were
going through. Sometimes I took short walks
around the motel and just let the tears go.
Other times I would turn the water on for a
shower or bath, so I could cry and not be
heard. I needed answers and the assurance
that help was on the way.

My body was fragmented. I had lost over eighty
percent of my body weight. The clothes that I
had worn before and during my pregnancy
were now too big. My muscles were still weak
from the weight of the baby without the
adequate balance to support me. My hair was
thin and I was constantly weak and fatigued. I
also knew that I was suffering from postpartum
depression. I was frustrated because I didn't
understand what I had gone through, and now I
had another human involved who was very
dependent on me. Upon the first visit to my

family doctor, I was told that it would be a year or more before I would be completely back to normal. Initial tests were run to check all of my hormone levels, and the tests came back showing dangerous vitamin deficiencies. I was placed on a vitamin regimen and a healthy diet for an adequate calorie count. My hormone imbalance was also believed to be the initial cause of my illness. Greater than my physical issues were my mental and emotional challenges. I was afraid to eat because of all of the vomiting. Even when I didn't "feel" that I was going to throw up, I still wanted to because I was used to vomiting by then. Memories of certain foods coming back up made me leery of what to eat, or if I really wanted to eat at all. I had to learn how to eat normal all over again. I felt sad and lost. I didn't want to question God, but I wanted to understand "why." I went to bed daily remembering what I'd just endured, and I woke up in the middle of the night panting and sweating from the nightmares. My doctor immediately suggested that I stay on antidepressants for an undisclosed period of time. I wouldn't take the antidepressants, because I didn't want to be numb from what I had gone through. Somehow I believed that feeling the weight of everything gave me a greater determination to overcome what I was going through. It also represented another opportunity for God to come down and soothe me when I felt that I couldn't take it anymore. My body was hurting, but my mind was still strong. My impatience for a true understanding of this trial caused me to feel an indifference towards God, but my deep love for Him wouldn't allow me to relinquish my loyalty. I wouldn't leave God; I decided to embrace Him so He could truly put me back together again. I reached out to a powerful intercessor whom I talked to at least twice a week, sometimes daily if the need was great. It helped to talk out my feelings and seek prayer support from someone who truly cared about me. God really met me during those sessions, and I was open to reconciling my relationship with Him. I felt His immeasurable love and healing touch come over me in fresh waves of joy. The pain of my heart was turning into gratitude because God saved my life and left me on Earth to serve His purpose. I hadn't died and left my family with only memories of me for the rest of their lives. I was alive and on the road to being well again. Shortly after this amazing connection with the "angel," my husband and I were blessed with a new vehicle and were approved for a new residence. The joy that filled our hearts was beyond any expression of words. The management and staff at the motel were sad to see us go, but happy that we were getting back on our feet again. They had been kind to us, and we were given wonderful baby gifts for Joshua from the staff. We announced

our move-in date to our new landlord and
returned to the motel to pack our things. Our
new house was not far from the motel, but we
had to make several trips to get everything.
Finally, we had a home to call our own.
Stepping into our new place truly felt like a new
beginning because a lot of the inner healing
had taken place back at the motel.

Finally, we were settled into our small, but cozy
place. There was nothing like sleeping in my
own bed. Part of the living room was set up as
the nursery. Joshua was sleeping longer, but
still getting up during the night. Terrence got up
with him to allow me to get the rest I needed,
and to heal. His selfless act was so honorable
of him since he was back to working his full
time schedule again. He got through his work
day by drinking a lot of coffee. We could not
afford child care, so I was home with the baby
during the day. I was still not well enough to

work.

Another part of my anxiety involved going to the bathroom. If I stayed in the bathroom longer than ten minutes or so, the painful memories of the violent vomiting came back, and I would start to panic. Sometimes even walking past the bathroom caused me to panic. Being alone during the day brought more awareness to the fact that I still had a long road to recovery. I had too much free time to think and dwell on things that were probably not in my best interest to think about. Despite it all, I made my living room a sanctuary to the Lord and would kneel by the sofa or sometimes stretch out on the floor to pray.

Chapter 9

Healing

I knew that the more I reached out to God, the further I would be from the pain. I have always been a worshipper and that alone has gotten me through some really tough times in my life. I would put on really soothing worship music or just sing myself into the presence of the Lord. Joshua would be napping, and at other times, he'd be lying in his bassinet observing his surroundings. I felt God's sweet embrace and knew that He was digging a well inside of me to give me more of Him. I became hungry and desperate to seek God more. I didn't have all of the answers, but I possessed the assurance that God was with me. This truth alone brought me great comfort and peace. God's love began to overshadow my fear and uncertainty.

The vomiting continued off and on for about six to eight months following Joshua's birth. I had a completely different body so it was necessary for me to purchase new clothes. My weight hadn't been that low since my single days before Donovan was born. My doctor ordered me to remain on the prescription drugs for my digestion because my esophagus was damaged and because of the erosion within the walls of my stomach. The overflow of acid had taken its toll over the months. My biggest challenge was regaining strength and mobility in my body so I could function the way I did before the pregnancy. The more that I rested, the more my body wanted to rest. I was also anemic, so any drastic changes in temperature became very uncomfortable to manage on a daily basis. Throughout this process, I had to exercise patience with God, with myself, and with others who had not been in my body to understand what I had gone through over the past year. Terrence had been with me, but did not completely understand the dynamics of what was going on inside of me. Looking back, I know that it was difficult for him to constantly hear me say, "I don't feel well."

We didn't know anyone where we lived so I struggled a lot to care for Joshua. The money wasn't there for Terrence to stay home all the time, so "toughing it out" became the routine.

The "honeymoon" period of staying in a motel where rent, utilities, and cable were rolled into one fee, was over. At our new place, we were responsible for rent and all of our utilities. Terrence ordered a small cable package so I could have something to keep me company as I was with Joshua all day. I researched programs to help with diapers and formula. Even though Terrence made an adequate salary, it was still not enough to cushion the blows of the financial crisis we'd endured, on top of the expenses of a new baby. Tension and stress became frequent visitors at our home. I was just not physically ready to return to work, and the idea of someone else caring for Joshua was out of the question. My quest was to find extra income that I could make while healing and being home with Joshua.

Chapter 10

A New Adventure

I stumbled upon an answer to our financial woes one day while walking through the local mall. I saw an Avon store, and I went in to look around. I decided to purchase a couple of things, and while checking out, the manager offered me an opportunity to become an Avon sales representative. The start-up costs were minimum, and I was approved to get started on my new adventure.

Terrence seemed hopeful and happy that I had found something that would bring in extra money. It had also given me a chance to get out again in public and make connections. Sitting in the house all day was not the most exciting thing in the world to do. Housework was one thing, but I've always felt more fulfilled when using my hands and brain. I had never been an idle person, but I'd always been goal-oriented and driven by success. Before long, I started to implement a plan to get my Avon books out and build my clientele. I targeted family, friends, neighbors, and businesses. It was actually a plus to have Joshua with me because most people were "taken" with him so that helped me a lot with sales. Within three months, I was in the top ten for sales as a new representative. My commission was good, but not always consistent. Some weeks were better than others. I began to travel a lot by car to meet new customers and to deliver the products. Honestly, I found more pleasure in just meeting people. It was quite challenging to juggle Avon plus an infant. Joshua slept through some stops, but at other times, he was fussy, and wanted my attention. I kept telling myself that I was doing it for the family. I wanted to feel like I was contributing to the household income. I'd even found a business to sell some of my bulk Avon products to on the weekends. It was a clothing store not too far from where we lived. The manager of the store allowed me to sell my products without charging me booth rent. Additionally, he didn't ask for a percentage of my sales. I showed my deep appreciation by offering him free products and giving him discounts on other products. Selling my products in that store only lasted for three months. I had to let it go because the store was located in a low income area. Most of the customers or inquirers wanted extra discounts on products, and I was often left with orders from previous campaigns. The district manager for my area was also starting to put more stress on the Avon reps to upsell everything. As much as I had overcome, I was still delicate. Extra pressure was not what I needed. A month or two before Joshua's first birthday, I canceled my status as an Avon representative. I was relieved and gave away

most of the products I had remaining.
Additionally, Terrence and I had been praying
to find a church in our area for a while. While
selling Avon products back at the store, I
connected with a lady who was a member of a
prophetic-apostolic ministry nearby. We
became part of that ministry, and that's where
additional inner healing took place. The prayer
warrior inside of me had been stirred and the
prophetic gifting had been awakened.

My physical appearance had changed because
of my illness, but a spiritual makeover was also
taking place. My love reservoir for God had
expanded. I was also more receptive and
compassionate towards the needs and pains of
others. God was pulling out of me what the
adversary thought he had emptied me of
through my trial. The Holy Spirit ignited a fire
deep within my soul. This fire was one that
would consume the residue of things past and

present; things that tried to prevent me from walking in my destiny.

Chapter 11

A Change of Lifestyle

Being sick for so long created a deep disdain within me for sickness. Any symptom of illness that tried to threaten me or my family immediately received a "death sentence." I began to study natural ways to prevent and heal common illnesses in my spare time. Although we didn't have a lot of extra money to buy supplements, I kept basic things on hand for natural remedies. I started shopping at the local farmer's market, because I wanted to incorporate more fruits and vegetables into our meals. God was using me in our home to be a change agent for a healthier lifestyle. Things were working out pretty well, and the family was much better for it.

Shortly after Joshua turned a year old, I ran into a lady who'd previously cared for Donovan when he was a year old. Bettye had a home daycare. It was great to see her again, and she became teary-eyed upon hearing about my life-threatening pregnancy. I was in her area one day and decided to stop by and visit with her. We had a great conversation, and the visit ended with her agreeing to watch Joshua a few days a week to give me a break. The price was too good to resist, and it was an answer to my prayers. Coupled with my ongoing recovery efforts over the last year, being with Joshua every day had been very difficult. It was causing a strain on my marriage because I had very little time to myself. When Terrence came home from work, I was always very tired and went to bed shortly after dinner. With a few days a week to myself, I could rest and be in a better mental state when my husband came home. I was missing the time that we would normally spend together. Having a second child had put a lot of strain on our relationship. Before Joshua was born, we'd had many date nights because of the shared custody with Donovan's dad. Now dates were very sporadic, and exhaustion became an unwelcomed guest in my body. Terrence agreed to the daycare arrangement, and we decided on the days that Joshua would be away for a few hours.

On the first day of daycare, I was nervous about leaving him. To my surprise, he settled in nicely and didn't cry when I prepared to leave. The first time I left Joshua at daycare, I didn't know what to do with myself. It felt so liberating to have some alone time; nevertheless, I adjusted pretty quickly and settled into getting things done before everyone arrived home. Joshua bonded pretty quickly with Ms. Bettye, and he also had other toddlers to play with at her home. Life began to get a lot easier for me because the burdens were being lifted from my shoulders.

At this point in my recovery, I had accepted the fact that I'd almost lost my life. I wasn't grieving anymore anytime this fact was brought up. I had started telling random people about the struggles I'd endured during my pregnancy. The responses I received were usually blank stares and awkward moments of silence. Sometimes I conveyed the details as a way to self-check how far I had come in my emotions and to keep things fresh in my memory. I had always known that one day I would be well enough to share my testimony. I was discovering the person I really was underneath all of the pain. It wasn't that I was a whole lot different than what I originally thought, but I was a lot stronger and had overcome more in life than I had given myself credit for. Pain was a prison, and I refused to serve a life sentence being in pain. Slowly, but surely I was well and whole again, despite all the blows life had dealt me.

Chapter 12

Going Back To School

When Joshua was about a year and a half old, I started to get the itch again to have a job or do something else outside of being a homemaker. In my former career, I had been an elementary school teacher for seven years in Ann Arbor Public Schools. My tenure as an educator had been cut short due to some unfortunate issues with parents. Honestly, I had been burned out with teaching for a while, so the backlash just helped me to pack my bags a lot sooner than I had expected. I didn't want to go back into a classroom, although it had been about five years since I resigned from my position. I had always wanted to get my master's degree and become a principal. My teaching days had taken up too much time, and I couldn't get comfortable with trying to go back to school while working a full time job. This was the perfect time for me to consider it while I was still home with the family. As I began to pray about it, the fire for pursuing the opportunity became ignited in my heart. I went to the library the next day to research masters' programs in education at local colleges in the area. Most of the schools required a test to get into graduate school, so I became a little discouraged as I researched my options. I felt like this was something I was supposed to do right away, not after waiting months to prepare for, and take a test. I left the library that day with a heavy heart. Upon getting into my car, I heard the soft voice of God say, "Marygrove." I started to get excited, and I rushed back into the library. I hadn't thought about that school. I had taught with a few colleagues who'd completed their programs at Marygrove. Marygrove was located in the Detroit area.

After logging onto the school's website, I discovered that the educational leadership program was due to start in just a few weeks. I called the school and requested that an information package be sent to me. To make things better, the program was online. I didn't have to travel to campus. All of my work could be done from the comfort of our home. I was so excited about this new adventure that I called Terrence at work to discuss the details. He was excited that I was so happy about everything. It was a plus to see me in this place after the emotional turmoil that I had experienced for so long. When the packet arrived in the mail, I completed my forms with haste. Additionally, there were additional documents to submit and an essay to write for consideration. I was confident that I would be accepted, and my dream of becoming a principal would become a reality. I was informed about an open house for potential students. I would have a chance to turn in my forms without a registration fee and also meet the staff of the education department. It was the happiest night of my life. I dressed for the occasion and met with the coordinator of the program. Soon after that delightful night, I received my acceptance letter in the mail. My financial aid had been approved and classes were due to start in May of 2012. I was officially a graduate student in the educational leadership program at Marygrove College. Terrence and I decided that I would go full-time so that I could finish the program within a year and a half. It would be a lot of work, but I was strong and determined. I had been given a second chance at life, and I was going to live out my dreams. Nothing and no one was going to stop me this time.

Just a few days short of starting classes, I started to panic and doubt that I would be able to handle school and a family at the same time. The classes in the program required a lot of writing and critical thinking. I hadn't been in school for years. What if I had forgotten the basics? Could I keep up with the work and maintain good grades? I also had never taken online classes before.

We had one week to complete the assignments, and I was taking two classes at a time. The reading, questions, and written papers were like a weekly climb up Mount Everest. I was thankful to have a supportive spouse who was my encouragement every step of the way. To my utter amazement, I finished with a 4.0 grade average for the first semester. I was ecstatic that my perseverance and hard work had paid off so soon. I was off to a great start, and creeping closer to my dreams. Nonetheless, all of the good news had me on the enemy's radar for an attack.

Chapter 13

Bad News

Within a month or so of me starting school, Terrence received a pink slip from his job of over six years. I remember the day I received the news. That day had proceeded as usual, and then I heard my phone ring. It was Terrence on the other line, and the tone of his voice immediately grabbed my attention. There was no need to ask what was wrong because it all came out. I couldn't say anything momentarily because of the huge lump in my throat. Basically, Terrence's department had experienced a reduction in funding and his current position would be eliminated within ninety days. We weren't prepared for a layoff. I had just started school, and there was only one source of income coming in. We hadn't fully rebounded from my illness. The questions started to drown my thoughts, but I had to remember that Terrence was still at work. There would be plenty of time to talk later. I hung up the phone in a melancholy mood. I was pretty frozen in my thoughts until Terrence came in from work. I asked him a lot of questions about what he had been told by his supervisor. To be completely honest, I was scared. Our income would be greatly reduced and there were no prospects for new employment in sight for either of us. I quickly revisited my status as a full time student, and suggested giving up the idea of school to return to work. Terrence was against the idea because I had already set my goal to be done with the program within a year and a half. Everything had come together so well for me to seize the opportunity, but I wanted him to know that I was willing to assist financially if I had to for the sake of our survival. I was willing to put my dreams on hold for the moment. It hurt for me to form the words "quit school", but I wasn't willing to sink financially because of my pride. At that point, we were almost three months behind on our rent because of unforeseen expenses. The plan was to contact agencies in the surrounding areas and see if we could get help with the back rent. We prayed like we had never prayed before, and believed for God's divine intervention in our circumstances. We received funds for the two months of rent from two different resources, but the other blow was that our rent was going up another $100 because of our lease ending. We didn't want to sign another lease because of the forthcoming layoff. Terrence's boss had given him a month's extension for his job. God's hand was certainly on us in spite of everything. A court ordered eviction was served to us because our rent was behind. We had no choice but to start packing our things. The corporate staff had given us an extra twenty four hours to vacate our apartment. We obtained a storage unit and rented a moving truck. Terrence and I finished packing everything and put it onto the truck. It was the hardest and the most painful day of my life. Reality had set in that we were homeless again. Our hope was that we would find a cheaper place to live within a few weeks. It just didn't happen that way. In the meantime, we were staying in motels here and there around the area. For the first time in our lives, we went to the human services office to obtain an application to apply for housing assistance, food stamps, and medical insurance. There was still no easy fix because the time frame to process the application was sixty days. We were also calling agencies to ask for assistance for places to stay that were income-based. In the world of human services, there is no such thing as urgency because everyone who applied had that same issue. The responses were slow and the options were limited. The stress of the situation set in and I started to feel overwhelmed. I was still in school at that point. It was hard to focus on school because I was worried about having a roof over our heads and food to eat. Additionally, we didn't have medical insurance anymore. I informed my professors about our situation, and they gave me extensions to turn in my work. The school's staff made phone calls trying to help us get a place in the Detroit area, but nothing worked out. I was beginning to feel like my professors expected me to quit school, but I wasn't going to give the adversary that advantage over me. If I quit, I would never complete the classes to get my master's degree. This period in time was one of those periods that I knew it was now or never. A lot was working against me, but I knew it would be worth the fight in the end, so I struggled to hang on daily.

Finally, after some time had passed, we received a letter regarding our food stamp application. We were awarded food stamps, but that was about it. Joshua was given full Medicaid benefits, but we didn't qualify for Medicaid based on the amount of unemployment payments we received. We were given the option of a spend down plan before Medicaid would even look in our direction. This was bad news considering my medical history. Being ill was definitely not in our plans. We didn't have the money to pay any doctor or hospital out of pocket for anything. We still didn't have anywhere to stay. We had to endure more waiting lists and conduct more searches online and in the papers. Terrence was looking for jobs day and night to supplement the income that he was receiving from the state. The desperation was setting in to find an affordable place to stay. The stress was starting to affect me to the point where I had to visit my doctor. I called beforehand to arrange a payment plan for the office visit. She wanted to put me on antidepressants again for the anxiety and insomnia, but I'd heard too many horror stories about those medications. Because of what I'd heard, I wasn't willing to take a chance on the possible side effects, and possibilities for an addiction.

In spite of everything, I was still maintaining a 4.0 grade point average. I was almost in my third semester of school. During the second semester, I'd accepted a few Incompletes in a couple of classes to give myself extra time to do the work. The best part was the extra time; the worst part was that I had to incorporate that extra work into my current schedule. The workload felt unbearable at times, but I pressed through because the fighter in me was swinging at every obstacle. Sometimes I swung through tears and anger; other times, it was through frustration. My refund checks from school helped us with living expenses and food costs, but the motel expenses were digging huge holes in our pockets on a weekly basis. We knew there had to be another way, but there was no real solution in sight. We stayed with some friends and family members here and there for a while, but that was no picnic. The beginning was great, but then things would always get too crowded and we all needed our space. There was no place like a home to call our own.

Chapter 14

Moving Into the Shelter

Terrence and I finally decided to pursue the one option that we had been trying to avoid for some time. There was no getting around it anymore, because we needed a place to stay that would allow us to keep money in our pockets and save up for a permanent residence. The option was living in a nearby family shelter. The idea of living in a homeless shelter was frightening, but there was nowhere else that we could turn for help. Terrence obtained a part time job at a nearby retail store, and he was starting work in the afternoons and getting off around eleven o'clock at night. Joshua and I were on our own to pass the time away until Terrence's work day was complete. I didn't attempt to study until after Terrence rejoined us because it was difficult to study alone with a toddler.

Eventually, we received a call that there was a room available for us at the shelter. After crying tears of fear, we gathered our things and moved in. Words can't begin to describe the experience of living in a shelter except to say that it was like living in a prison. There were so many rules that we had to live by. Additionally, constantly being searched upon coming into the shelter topped my long list of dislikes. No outside food was allowed in and any medication brought in required a doctor's note. Since it was a family shelter, every room was assigned "house chores" to be completed before bedtime. Of course, I was responsible for our chores because Terrence worked in the evening. I had the lovely job of cleaning the women's restroom. Bleach wasn't strong enough to kill the amount of filth in that place.

Blood, feces, hair, and puke were commonplace. I had to bring Joshua with me because he wasn't allowed to stay in the room alone. Full compliance to every rule was required because failure to adhere to any of the posted rules could result in us being put out of the shelter. I passionately hated living in a shelter, but I kept telling myself that living there was only temporary. My smallest window of sanity was being out during the day and leaving to go pick up my husband from work at night. There were a couple of Christian families that we connected with while living there, but besides that, we decided it was best if we kept to ourselves. The good news was that we were moving up on the housing waiting lists because we were in a shelter. The down side was being treated poorly and the shelter's attempts to control us because of our financial situation. We weren't like most of the families who lived there, because we had college degrees. Living in a shelter was an unfortunate decision that we had to make because of an unexpected layoff.

We were required to meet with our assigned social worker on a weekly basis. I gritted my teeth to sit in those meetings because of the invasive questions she often asked. I assumed they believed we were like many of the people who lived in the shelter: liars, addicts, or victims of abuse. I was concerned about us staying healthy more than anything else because the facility was not clean. Sometimes, it smelled like a nursing home, and other times, it smelled like a daycare. I didn't allow Joshua to go into the play areas with the other children because I feared he'd contract something that would make him sick. There were no televisions in the rooms, only my laptop computer where we occasionally watched a movie. The shelter had a small library and a computer lab. The internet connection was limited and did not always work. Completing my schoolwork was a challenge because of the faulty internet connection. I had to go to the public library to complete my school work, and Joshua didn't always give me the time I needed to focus. I missed having a normal life. If I had ever taken anything in my life for granted before, this was my lesson to never do it again. I missed going in and out of rooms, having a refrigerator to go into for whatever I wanted, having a private bathroom, and enjoying the privacy to have heart-to-heart conversations with my husband. Terrence and I had our deepest talks on the way to drop him off at work. We weren't comfortable having a lot of our conversations while at the shelter because we were constantly being scoped and monitored by the staff. I knew that some of the people at the shelter had a problem with us, so I was always on my warfare watch. I didn't sleep well on the cots in the room. My dreams were full of turmoil and fright. I prayed over our room on a daily basis and asked God to cover us. In my mind, this was the absolute lowest that I had been in my entire life.

Chapter 15

Looking For the Good

I tried to practice looking for the good in our circumstances. We were very blessed to have our own transportation. Most of the families in the shelter had to rely on others to get them around or catch the city bus. We had money coming in from unemployment and a part time job. Others did not have any income coming in, and they were looking for jobs. While out during the day, I drove around the really nice neighborhoods and allowed my mind to run ramped with thoughts of a brighter future. The food that we were served at breakfast, lunch, and dinner was supplied through donations. Whether the food would be edible or not was a gamble. There were bedtime snacks served for the families, and these snacks were usually fattening or sugary. The winding down of each day meant we would be one day closer to a solution that would free us from that place. Due to our income, the only available option was to apply for public housing. We couldn't afford market rent. The days were going by fast, but the responses from the waiting lists were pouring in slowly. The Christmas holiday was quickly approaching, and various churches and organizations were coming in to do special crafts with the kids and to provide treats for the families. Honestly, the holidays were some of the best days to enjoy eating again. I felt I was being served as a human being and not as an animal. We were given nice gifts as well.

Many of the residents of the shelter were being kicked out for fighting or breaking other rules. There was always that fear in the back of my mind that we were next to go. Terrence and I were working overtime to look for housing and better jobs. There were just no solid leads at that time. The only thing we could do at that time was keep hope alive and continue to press towards better days. Additionally, I hadn't seen much of Donovan during those trying times. I just couldn't bring him into the shelter because I was embarrassed, and I felt like I'd failed as a parent to provide for him. I justified my actions by telling him that we were getting repairs done on our place, someone was sick, and the list went on. I just couldn't tell Donovan the truth right then. I would unload everything when the time was right. The disappointment in his voice was heartbreaking. Many times, he'd hang up the phone on me or speak bitterly towards me from his frustration. Donovan was safe in the care of his dad, and that alone brought me great comfort.

The winter weather set in and the winds were bitter. Going out late to pick Terrence up from work often involved driving slowly through blinding snow. Bundled up and warm, Joshua would fall sound asleep in his car seat. I had my thoughts and the road conditions to contend with all by myself. I hummed along to Christmas music or used the time to pray. In my opinion, every day completed was another obstacle that we had overcome.

In this very dark pit of hopelessness and despair was a glimmer of light. A few weeks before we'd lost our place, I was on campus and came across a great opportunity. I had seen a flyer posted about opportunities to study abroad as a Marygrove student. Undergraduate and graduate students were encouraged to apply. There were several cities listed, but the one that stuck out to me was Paris, France. I started to close my eyes and picture myself there. What an amazing city and how memorable it would be for me to experience the beauty of what I had seen on television and in pictures. I decided to go to the office of the director of the programs. She was out, but her assistant gave me some brochures and encouraged me to attend the upcoming informational meeting. Of course, the part of me that was in touch with reality started to override my excitement for a new adventure. The trip would cost over three thousand dollars, and of course, spending money for souvenirs and meals were not included. My faith was in charge, so I attended the informational meeting. The presentation sold me in every way, and I had a chance to ask additional questions. I was the only graduate student in attendance and would likely be the only graduate student traveling to France with undergraduate students and staff leaders. I would have to take a class to prepare me for the trip because this was not a pleasure trip. There would be some down time, but I would be responsible for work before, during, and after the journey. One of the professors suggested I incorporate my studies to be a principal into my assignments. I met with my coordinator, and we agreed that I could study the French education system while there. I would just have to figure out who I could talk to and make the connection. I would be given a nice amount of points to count towards the internship hours needed for graduation. This was a chance of a lifetime, but the problem was that there was a deposit due to hold my place in the group and secure my plane ticket. The required deposit was around two hundred dollars, in addition to getting a passport and the things I might need to bring along with me. I took some time to be honest with God and laid the desire before Him. We didn't have the money for the deposit, but my heart was determined to pursue this life-changing experience. There was a deadline to pay the deposit. I continue to pray about it, and search my brain for a solution.

The date to pay the deposit was just a few days away, so I decided to talk with the director about my dilemma. To my utter amazement, my deposit was covered, and I only had to purchase my passport. There was an essay contest, and a passport would be the prize. I put together my essay and turned it in by the deadline. I knew that God was in this plan, and He wasn't going to let me down. A few weeks later, I was given the amazing news that I had won the contest, and the passport was placed in my hand. I almost passed out in the office.

Chapter 16

Good News

It was official. I was going to study abroad in Paris, France during the spring break vacation of the following year. In the midst of the heartbreaking layoff and the loss of our home, God had restored my hope by giving me an amazing miracle. I held onto this in my heart during the dark days at the shelter. I wasn't going to forfeit my trip because of the lack of finances and a home. It would work out and my family would be at a permanent residence while I was out of the country for ten days. I wanted to scream it to the world that I was going to France, but I kept it locked away. Our case worker knew that I was a full-time student, but that's all she knew. Terrence and I had never discussed the trip while residing there. The only time we discussed the trip was when and if we were far away from itching ears.

Our France group had a pizza and candy fundraiser to raise funds for the trip. I had a few orders that had been delivered to me prior to our circumstances taking a turn for the worse. Christmas Day at the shelter had arrived. We had many packages to open from the many generous people who had taken the time to have us make a list of our needs and wants for the holidays. Nevertheless, there was still a cloud of sadness in my heart that the gifts hadn't chased away. We received our usual holiday texts from family and friends. No one knew that we were in a shelter because we had always chosen to live very private lives. Our past experiences of revealing too much to people had proved to be a bigger cross to bear than the trial itself. There are just some things in life that are better left unsaid until we are on the other side of them. I learned to speak more about what I'd conquered and to speak less about what I was currently battling. Life was more peaceful that way.

Christmas day was quiet. There wasn't much to do because everything was closed down. We were allowed to leave and stay out later than usual, but there wasn't much to do. Pouring over gifts and taking a few naps made the day go by as though it had never arrived in the first place. That was fine with me because I wanted it to end quickly. Joshua was enjoying his new toys and was oblivious to the faint ache of disappointment in the air. Christmas dinner was pretty decent, but I wasn't really in the mood to eat. I had begun to lose weight because of the poor diet selection and the deep anxiety that I had been struggling with over the weeks. I put on my face of strength when outside of our room, but behind the doors I gave way to my tears. I was fighting to believe that God hadn't forgotten us. The encouragement that I received from friends gave me the strength to be patient for a positive outcome, and I had to pull on that strength daily. My tears were of a sweet surrender to the mercy of God. He had yanked me out of the clutches of death, and I knew He would show Himself strong again on my behalf.

It was now 2013, and the New Year came in with us taking a few days in a hotel to ourselves. It was nice to be in a different environment that wasn't constrained and guarded all of the time. The residents were given what I referred to as a "get out of jail free" card. We had a couple of days to spare before returning to the "dungeon" by the usual curfew. We didn't know it at the time, but there was another tidal wave headed our way.

Chapter 17

Another Blow

The tidal wave hit the week at the start of the winter semester at Marygrove. We headed out to drop Terrence off to work. As I approached the car, I noticed that all of the windows were foggy. I opened the driver's door, and a cloud of smoke enveloped my face. Terrence was lagging behind me so I turned around and yelled for his attention. The car was on fire! Terrence hurried over and opened the trunk and more smoke met our faces. Terrence grabbed his phone and called 911. The fire crew came, but the damage had already been done. The articles of clothing, CDs, and Joshua's car seat were all ruined from smoke damage. The color of the interior was now a dull burnt brown. The smell of the charred

material was nauseating. After a brief
investigation, it was determined that the fire
likely started from the trunk of the car, but there
was no clear evidence as to the cause of the
fire. We took Joshua back inside of the building
to stay with a staff member who was working in
the front office. We wanted to keep him out of
harm's way. My backpack for school was in the
back seat and was completely damaged. My
books were still useable, but the backpack had
to be disposed of. Terrence and I reeked of
smoke and were covered in soot. From what
we had been told, the car was gone. There
would be nothing that could be done to recover
it from the smoke damage. The firefighters who
came out gave us a small check towards the
purchase of a new car. We gave them our
information so they could put us in contact with
some organizations that would probably be
able to help us with new transportation.
Terrence called his job to give his supervisor

the news and to report his absence from work
that day. My heart was bleeding, and the tears
began to pour down my soot-stained face. I
called my mentor to solicit her prayers and to
soak up new encouragement. Terrence
assured me that he would do everything he
could to see if the car could be salvaged from
the smoke damage. It was a very difficult time
for us to be without a car. Terrence's job was a
good distance away and there was no quick
solution for how we could get him there and
back to the shelter. Although we cleaned
ourselves thoroughly, the smoke was still
lingering around us. The other residents
wanted to know what had happened, and we
shared the news with them. It was a tiring and
somber rest of the day. There was nothing to
do but rest up so that our minds could go to
work for solutions. We reported the fire to the
staff and were told that our car would have to
be removed very soon. Broken or damaged

cars were not allowed on county property. After about two weeks of grueling phone calls, we found a guy who owned a garage where the car's interior could be cleaned thoroughly for possible restoration. There was no definite time frame for how long it would take, but at least hope was on the horizon. Selling the car to a junkyard was a rip off because no one was offering much for it. All we could do was settle in and pray for a miracle.

In the meantime, Terrence was catching the shelter van and the public transit system to work. His supervisor was kind enough to bring him back at night. There was a small shopping center within walking distance if we wanted something different or extra to eat outside of the daily meals we were served at the shelter. It was becoming a habit for us to walk in the shelter's cafeteria and walk back out because the meals weren't edible. The only other options we had were meals from the nearby grocery store, Subway, or McDonald's.

Not having our own transportation was putting a halt on our plans to look for housing and other employment. We were able to catch rides here and there, but we were still waiting to hear the progress on the car. All we knew was that the car was being stripped and cleaned. Only time would tell if the charred smell could be removed so the car could be driven again. We rented a car for a couple of days to take care of some important business matters. I can't put into words the pleasure of being on the road again. The rental car was a newer model with a new car smell. One day, we received word that our current vehicle would be ready within the week for pick up. The Lord had worked another miracle for us. He blessed us to find that garage and pay for the car to be thoroughly detailed without spending a lot of money. He

Another Blow

had come through once again.

Chapter 18

A New Beginning

A friend in Toledo, Ohio offered to let us live with him. Terrence was reluctant at first, so he'd placed the idea on the back burner, but I was beyond sick of living in a shelter, and I wasn't eating or sleeping well. I began to experience small anxiety attacks because of the living conditions at the shelter, in addition to worrying about being evicted from the shelter. If we decided to live with our friend, we would have a temporary place to stay in Toledo until we found a place of our own. After all, Terrence was still receiving unemployment and could always look for another job there. I was ready to go without hesitation, but I was frustrated because Terrence was slightly uncomfortable. At that point, I began to nag him a lot. He didn't

want to move without having a job already
lined up. I was willing to take a leap of faith;
one that would give us peace of mind, more
nutritious meals, and an opportunity for a new
beginning. I wasn't doing well physically or
emotionally, and I didn't want to have a
nervous breakdown. Our friend informed us
that if we decided to move forward, he would
travel from Ohio to help us move our things
because our car wasn't quite ready to be
picked up yet.

Finally, we decided that Sunday of the
upcoming week would be our last day at the
shelter. I could hardly hide my excitement, but
we carried on as usual so that none of the staff
would suspect anything and try to kick us out
sooner. When Terrence went to work, I would
organize and pack our things. I was starting to
feel better because the end of our days living in
a shelter was clearly in sight. Terrence and I

floated through our weekly meeting with our social worker. Nothing else seemed relevant at that point, but the reality of it all would soon be known to everyone. We planned to take only the possessions we had with us, and we'd continue to pay the monthly rent for the storage unit that was holding the rest of our things. Terrence notified his supervisor that we were leaving. At one point in time, Terrence and his manager had spoken of him transferring to a store in Toledo, but it never happened. We continued to prepare for departure as the week was coming to an end. Our friend would be arriving Sunday afternoon to pick us up. After we finished packing early Sunday morning, we went to the front office of the shelter and announced to the staff member on duty that we were officially leaving the premises. Of course, the staff member asked us a bunch of questions and tried to get us to change our minds; nevertheless, we signed the paperwork for release. Some of the other residents found out that we were leaving, and came in to give us their well wishes. After a couple of trips back and forth to the car, it was finally time to get on the road. I was so relieved that we were leaving that I slept most of the way.

We arrived in Toledo late that evening. The joys of having freedom to come and go as we pleased, buying and preparing our own food, and talking about things when we wanted to was simply a delight. I slept like a baby for the first time in a few months. I hadn't awakened in the middle of the night because of a nightmare or panic attack. It was rest from Heaven.

We spent the next few weeks getting to know the new area, and Terrence started looking for employment. We had also received a call that our car was ready to be picked up, and our friend gave us a ride back to Michigan to pick up our vehicle. The car looked awesome. The interior had been cleaned very thoroughly. There was still a hint of the smoke smell in the air, but we knew that in time, it would all be gone. It was a miracle to have our car back, and we were overjoyed as we traveled back to Ohio.

We were settled in a new state, and we had to make it official. We began to pursue getting our Ohio driver's licenses and new plates for the car. After seeking out information regarding proper documentation, we planned to move forward once we received our tax refund. Toledo was a slower, quieter city, and that was just what we needed after being in an uptight and stressful situation for so long. The area we moved to was near the University of Toledo campus and offered a variety of restaurants and shopping centers, but employment was still an issue. Terrence wasn't finding a job as fast as he'd planned. We still had a little income coming in, but we needed more money to keep up with our bills and obtain a permanent residence. Our payment for the storage unit in Michigan was getting behind again, so we called the company to set up payment arrangements, but the amount was still too overwhelming. Of course, if we got too far behind, the unit would be taken over by management and our belongings would be auctioned off to the public. Terrence and I attempted to hold on for a while, but one day, we were suddenly at peace with letting everything go. We had more important issues that required our attention, and material things could always be replaced at a later date. We had also reconnected with our church in the area, and Donovan was visiting us again on the weekends.

As time went along, Terrence secured

employment in the marketing field. It was a very new kind of work for him, and the hours were long. He didn't get off until after ten at night, and he had to work on Saturdays. He was initially told by his job manager that he would be getting a reasonable hourly pay on top of commission, but the bulk of his check came through securing sales. Neither of us was thrilled about this, but it was a rest stop on the way to something better. Terrence was trying to continue with the company in hopes of moving up to a management position. The potential in him for advancement was there, but the patience to get there wasn't. We were a family of four, and the commission-only pay was not feasible for us to survive and move forward with our future goals. I still had a few more months before I would be done with school. After a grueling three months of working and giving things his best efforts, Terrence resigned from his position at the marketing firm. We talked it over a few days prior to his resignation and agreed that this was the best decision for us. Money from school and our taxes had given us a cushion. This gave us the time needed to revisit our options and consider other employment opportunities.

Chapter 19

Leaving For France

I started my travel seminars in preparation for my trip to France. I drove to Detroit for a number of Saturdays and stayed in the seminars for a few hours. I was bored with the class and the assignments, but I was excited about meeting the members of the team. My roommate was an adjunct professor at Marygrove. She was a classy and a very high strung lady. My trip expenses were paid in full, and Terrence had given me spending money for meals and souvenirs. The time frame in which we received our tax refund and the date of our departure was simply the sovereignty of God. His hands were certainly on that trip and on my life.

The day for the grandest adventure of my life
arrived, and Terrence drove me to Marygrove
to catch the shuttle to the airport. It felt like only
yesterday when my life was hanging in the
balance, and suddenly, I was a graduate
student on my way out of the country for ten
days. Terrence had been hired at another job,
but he wasn't due to start work until after I
returned to the United States.

Our flight to Paris was six hours long, and we
left at night. Our airline was Air France, and all
of the flight crew was French. There were
televisions on the plane to watch shows and
movies. I slept on the way there and woke up
to the bright sunshine radiating through the
little windows. We were only an hour or so
away, and I was extremely excited. When we
landed, I felt as if I was in a dream. There were
about twenty-five of us on the team, and we
quickly got our bags to move toward boarding

the motor coach with our tour guide. Some people exchanged their money at the airport, but I decided to wait for another opportunity at a better rate. I was a little concerned about my money lasting for the duration of the trip, but I just prayed to God and asked for His continuous provision and protection over my life. We were finally on our way to have lunch, visit the Eiffel Tower, and check into our hotel. The first day was long and tiring. Our hotel rooms were beautiful, but tiny. Our room faced the courtyard, and the view was breathtaking. I felt like I could sit in front of the window for hours. Breakfast was included in our accommodations, and we were in walking distance of restaurants, small shops, parks, and the metro train station. Most of our mornings began very early, and the days ran late into the evening. The jet lag was overwhelming the first day. I felt like a walking zombie trying to figure out where I was and what I was doing. It was very cold in France at that time of the year, so dressing appropriately was important. Once we reached our destination from the metro station, we walked for the rest of the day. A lot of the group members started to complain about having sore feet and being tired, but we'd been warned about the excessive walking. Paris was everything that I had seen on television, in books, and heard about from other people. It was indeed the most beautiful city that I had ever visited in my life. There was a pretty strict itinerary to adhere to on a daily basis. The architecture, food, sights, history, culture, and the people were simply exquisite. It was unlike anything I had ever experienced before on Earth. I didn't speak a lot of French prior to the trip, but that wasn't a big issue. We were given a list of common phrases to use, but I soon discovered that I knew more than I realized. The French people weren't hard on foreigners

who didn't know the language, as long as they
were kind and pleasant. The food tasted great
and was definitely different from American
food. The portions were large, but not
overdone or heavy. That was the only time I
had ever been able to eat a full course meal
with dessert. After the meal, I didn't feel as
though I had overeaten. I loved the tap water,
soda, and the freshly squeezed orange juice in
the morning at the hotel. It was all fresh and
didn't taste overly processed and sugary like
products from the United States. The most
difficult part about being away from home was
the time difference. I had to stay up late to talk
with my family back in Ohio. I purchased an
international phone plan, so I was text
messaging during the day and calling to talk
with Terrence at night. I also called Donovan
and checked in on him every couple of days.
Donovan didn't like the fact that I was so far
away, but I assured him that I was safe and

would be home soon. Truthfully, there wasn't a lot of time to miss my family except at night during the down time and when things were quiet. I didn't sleep very well at the hotel, because it was a strange place with different sounds. We were arriving back at the hotel relatively late most nights, so we were able to rest briefly before the time came to get up and start moving again. There was a little free time during the day, and I spent it exploring or shopping with other group members. Some of the ladies were really going out and buying very expensive things like purses, jewelry, and shoes. We were warned before we left to be very aware of our surroundings and to watch out for pickpockets who enjoyed preying on tourists. Being observant had never been an issue for me because I was always paying close attention to people and where they were in proximity to me. One of the girls ended up getting some things stolen from her while we were out one day, but the theft could have easily been prevented if she'd followed directions. The red areas for pickpockets were the Eiffel Tower, the Louvre museum, and on the metro. A thief's favorite areas were mostly the places that were typically filled with distractions, and had issues with overcrowding. I just prayed and kept my eyes open. I ended up being the one warning the others about suspicious activity that I observed. I think my build and height deterred anyone from bothering me, as well as the angels of the Lord who was always close by. There were very few days of sunshine in Paris, but when they came in, they were very bright. Other than that, the weather was a gray overcast with drizzle and brisk winds. It was very difficult at times to battle the elements while walking. I tried to dress in layers and take my allowed breaks to warm up. My money stretched further than I imagined it would go because God continued to show me His faithfulness to keep me and provide for my needs. There were people who offered to buy some of my meals, and anytime I looked in my purse, more money was available.

The week of our stay in Paris was also the fashion week. We walked past the venues where many of the celebrity fashion designers were holding their events. It was rumored that Chanel, the designer, was in Paris at that time. It was pretty amazing how comfortable I was in such an amazing country. I didn't feel like a foreigner or indifferent because I am African American. For the first time in my life, I hadn't experienced racism. As I ventured into upscale shops, no one looked down on me or followed me around because of a preconceived notion that I would steal something from them. I kept opening and closing my eyes and pinching myself because what I was experiencing was nothing short of magical. During one of our group luncheons, I ate duck for the first time. It tasted a lot like chicken, only a little tougher in texture, and it left a greasy aftertaste. French cuisine consisted of heavier sauces and gravies with the main course. Of course, every meal was served with bread. It was also common to eat cheese with any dessert. I noticed that the French were a lot more conscious about being respectful and showing good manners to others. It was considered rude to enter a shop without first greeting the owner, and the same was expected upon departure. The family structure seemed a lot more balanced because both parents were often present with their children in public places. At other times, I saw fathers out with their kids, pushing the baby strollers or assisting the older children as they rode their bicycles on the sidewalks. Meal times in the French culture, particularly dinner, started late and ended even later because of the importance of family time. Conditions in children such as Attention Deficit Hyperactivity Disorder (ADHD) were thought by French psychologists to be treated first by examining the family structure for evidence of emotional strains or dysfunction; whereas, in the United States, ADHD is usually treated with medications. I was convinced that Paris would be one of the places I wanted to bring my family to for frequent visits.

On our last full day in Paris, which was also considered our "free day", I was scheduled to meet with an educational adviser from Fulbright France prior to our departure back to the United States. It had been very challenging to set a meeting up because of the language barrier, skepticism about dealing with a foreign student, and the fact that most of the French schools were out on a holiday break. Finally, I was able to set up an appointment with the French adviser. This meeting was the highlight of my trip because I would be creating a PowerPoint presentation from my research that would count towards my internship hours. The goal was to examine the strengths and weaknesses of the French versus American's educational systems. I had prepared interview questions beforehand to ask the adviser. The interview was scheduled for the afternoon, but I left with one of the faculty members to get an early start on the journey. It was a gloomy and a rainy day, and I would have loved to remain at the hotel and take a nap, but I knew that this was my only chance to get the interview done before we left for the United States. We stopped along the way at a bakery to get a sandwich, and after that, we went back to the metro station.

After we left the metro, we'd walked a long way

before stopping at a hair salon to ask for clarity on directions. Finally, we reached the building of our destination and rang the doorbell. The faculty leader waited in the library while I went upstairs to meet with the adviser. The meeting went well, and I gathered a lot of information to include in my presentation. After leaving Fulbright France, we realized how late it was, so we started heading to the restaurant where we were meeting as a group for our farewell dinner. Finding the restaurant was no easy task because we didn't know the exact address of the restaurant. After making a few phone calls, catching a cab, walking for a number of miles, and stopping a few times to ask for directions, we finally arrived at the restaurant. We were over an hour late so the rest of the group had eaten most of their main course. The restaurant was booming and crowded, and the sounds of music were fantastic. My emotions were all over the place because I knew I would miss Paris, but I was ready to go home to be with my family.

Chapter 20

Home Sweet Home

The dinner celebration came to an end and most of us headed back to the hotel. Some of the other group members went to a club and partied until the wee hours of the night. My roommate and I stayed up late to pack our things. We wanted to be ready before checkout the next morning. The plan was to have breakfast, and then gather in the lobby to wait on the motor coach that would take us to the airport. We were told to be at the airport at least two hours before our flight.

The next day was chaotic as we scurried to prepare for checkout. It was difficult to get everyone out of the hotel and onto the bus. We arrived at the airport late, and had to endure a nerve-racking process of trying to retrieve our board passes, go through the security check, clear customs, and finally arrive at the gate for departure. I was ready to get the flight over and done with so I could be home sweet home. The trip back to the United States seemed lengthier than the trip to France. I watched television and drifted in and out of sleep. We were served two meals and a snack while aboard, and all of it tasted like wax and cardboard. I forced myself to remain seated, and I adjusted my posture frequently to keep my legs from falling asleep. There wasn't much to do because it was a full flight. I was very hungry and planned on taking a chance on airport food once we landed in Detroit. I knew I was back in America when I noticed that the officers at customs were curt and rude. Our bags were sniffed by dogs, and if our bags had any food in them, they were randomly searched by security. Thankfully, I hadn't brought any food from

France, only souvenirs. A lot of the other group members purchased and packed beverages and food, so their clearance time took a lot longer. I was finally able to relieve my bladder and grab something light to eat. I headed towards the tiny office by the exit to exchange my money back to American dollars, and after that, I was off to board the shuttle for the ride back to the campus. It was a sad ending to a great adventure. I had bonded with the rest of the group, and I would sincerely miss seeing and interacting with everyone. My heart started pounding as we inched closer to Marygrove. I couldn't wait to hug Terrence and the boys. The thought of seeing their faces and talking to them in person brought a few tears to my eyes. As the shuttle pulled up, I could see our car parked. Once the shuttle parked, I said goodbye to the other group members and headed straight for the loving arms of my family. We had so much to talk about, so the trip back to Ohio was filled with good food and great conversation. I was tired and jet lagged for at least a week following the trip. My family enjoyed their gifts from France, and they enjoyed hearing the stories of all the adventures I took while I was there. I began to feel down and lost, but didn't know how to express how I felt. I was trying to get back to my normal life in America with my family, but I was functioning like a robot and not a person. After speaking with the assistant to the international programs at Marygrove, I found out that what I was experiencing was called culture shock. I was told it would pass, but was common with people who've traveled to other countries for extended periods of time. I was emotional and longed in my heart to return to Paris. Terrence was patient and allowed me to work through my emotions. When I felt overwhelmed, I tried to talk things out versus isolating myself from the family. The "shock" didn't go away overnight, but it got better with time. It became easier to look at pictures and souvenirs without experiencing a huge lump in my throat.

I went over my notes from the interview with the adviser, and put together my PowerPoint presentation. I emailed my presentation to the instructor and received an "A" for the assignment. I felt a sense of satisfaction and completion that all had gone well with my French adventure. A few weeks after the trip, all of the students from the study abroad trip got together for a dinner. The program assistant asked me and two other group members who'd went to France to share a brief overview of our experiences in France.

Chapter 21

Back to Reality

The focus was back to our new life in Ohio. Terrence and I filed for state benefits and housing assistance. Coming from a homeless shelter to a new state helped us with getting assistance a lot faster. We were moved to the top of the waiting list, and we qualified for a few other programs that assisted with furniture and other household needs. We had lost everything from our storage unit back in Michigan.

Of course, our application to receive additional benefits ran into some snags, but I saw it as another opportunity to trust God. After two months of residing in Toledo, our benefits were approved and a door for housing opened up for us. We visited the property and had many reservations about moving in, but our rent was income-based, and we would have a chance to recover from the financial devastation we'd suffered over the last few months. We made our decision and went in to sign the lease. We started moving that same day and took most of the evening to move our possessions from our friend's house into our new residence. We had more possessions than we knew, but they were mostly clothes and shoes. We bought a few more necessary household items. At the time of our move-in, we had no furniture except for an air mattress and one large television. Our application to receive furniture from a program that helped low-income families obtain furniture was processed shortly thereafter, but we would have to wait at least a month before our appointment. As empty as our place looked, there was a peace in my heart that we were on the road to recovery. We knew our situation was temporary and our place wouldn't always look the way it looked. Terrence was back to work, but it was an on-call job as a quality inspector. Work was slow at first, but it eventually started to pick up. Terrence went from working one or more days a week to five or more days a week. The pay wasn't the best, but the paychecks were consistent and the job was steadier than the previous marketing position. The job paid hourly, so we knew what to expect every two weeks based on the number of hours that Terrence worked at the factory. Terrence's unemployment benefits had dried up, so the need to trust God was even greater than before. I won't say I didn't have fears or doubts repeatedly overriding my faith; I did at many times. We had no one to go to for help but God. It took us about five or six months before we were in a position to adequately furnish our place, but during the time when we didn't have furniture, we sat, ate, and slept on air mattresses. When Donovan came over, he would repeatedly ask me when he was going to get his own bed. I didn't have a definite answer, so I told him things were going to look better very soon, even though I was having a hard time believing my own words. When my faith wanted to give out, hope kicked in to jumpstart my patience in God's timing again. I started applying for jobs to help out again, but nothing definite had been offered to me. School continued to go on and I was still doing well in all of my classes. I was learning how to be thankful in some things when I wanted to become impatient with others. We were blessed to be getting help from the State of Ohio through food stamps, some cash assistance, and medical insurance. Before this time, only Joshua had been insured.

Finally, we had a nice place to stay without having to share with other families. We didn't have the funds to buy the most expensive food or clothes, but there were organizations that helped us, and most times the items were free. Every day offered another opportunity for us to get better and for God to move miraculously on our behalf. I would pray and ask for His direction on where to go for things, and I would be led to call someone, or while I was out, I would stop by wherever God led me. Whatever need we had would be supplied on that same day or at least by the next day. We were walking through a wilderness experience, but God was providing our daily manna. I was learning how to pray and allow God to provide for us His way and not my way. God was also stretching my capacity to truly care about others and to not feel that I was better or above someone else. The bonus of living in Toledo was the cost of living was a lot lower than Michigan. The gas prices were cheaper, and we saved tons of money on our car insurance because Ohio is an at-fault state. My next item of business was to find childcare for Joshua for at least a few days a week. This endeavor was more nerve-racking and meticulous because I didn't really know anyone in Toledo. I received a couple of referrals to look into, and I proceeded to check them out. The first daycare provider was more expensive, but provided a lot of educational opportunities for Joshua. As I spoke with the woman over the daycare, I noticed that Joshua wouldn't interact with her. He sat on my lap the whole time and wouldn't get up to walk around or to check things out. I saw this as a bad sign because if he wasn't comfortable, I wouldn't be comfortable leaving him there all day. I thanked the provider for her time, and we left. A couple of weeks later, I set up an appointment to meet with another referral to tour her daycare. After arriving at the lady's home, Joshua warmed up very quickly to her and started interacting with her. The price was affordable, the daycare wasn't far from where we lived, and I was very comfortable with the place. I retrieved the paperwork to finalize the agreement for Joshua to start within the week. A week turned into a few months because it was difficult for me to think about leaving Joshua in a stranger's care. I had been very protective of him since the day he was born, and this time was no different for me. Eventually, I had no choice but to leave him at daycare because of my schoolwork and Terrence's work schedule. He was working mostly afternoons and nights, so I had to care for Joshua and try to juggle everything else. It became overwhelming and tiring, and I didn't have a lot of time to myself to recover. I had forgotten how toddlers had endless energy and very high demands. After a few months, Terrence started working six days a week. Sunday had become his only day off. I was beginning to feel my patience being stretched as I endured the process. I didn't have joy in walking the faith path every day, but there was something deep down inside me that pushed me to persevere. Terrence's work hours kept going back and forth. Life had started to feel like a seesaw, and I was trying very hard not to get dizzy and fall off. The further we went, the more I could see God's hand on us. God was helping me progress in my development as a person and a future leader. The back and forth, the ups and downs, and the uncertainties were teaching me how to respond God's way and how to keep my eyes steady on Him. It was only when I took my eyes off God that I dealt with the discouragement and the "dizziness" of life. I was being stripped of total reliance on myself and others. In spite of it all, I continued to believe God would allow me to reach my destination safely. He would take me to my place of purpose in Him. It was difficult not seeing my husband for long periods of time because he was working ten to twelve hours shifts, but the time away taught me to appreciate the time we had together. The petty things didn't mean as much anymore because we were always catching up on what was happening in one another's lives.

Chapter 22

Living the Dream

Most of the master's program was behind me so my new focus was finding an internship at a kindergarten through twelfth grade school. I would be on my own because I didn't have any connections in Ohio.

My last semester of classes would be the fall semester of 2013. My goal was to have my internship done by then. I would have two classes left to complete in addition to the internship. I had a number of contacts to turn me down, and then I acquired a solid lead from a friend of mine, but when I called the school I wanted to do the internship with, they said they hadn't heard from my friend. I was well into the fall semester of school with no internship in sight. I decided that I had no choice but to complete my internship during the winter semester of 2014. The delay was a huge disappointment because I had placed myself on a time frame. It really didn't matter because Marygrove had only one graduation per year. I would only be able to walk in May of 2014. I sent out emails to two high school principals, and one of them responded within a day. I called the school and made an appointment to be interviewed by the principal. I was nervous because that meeting would be my only opportunity to make a good first impression and land an internship. After taking my final two classes, I became very grateful that my internship had not become an additional workload because those classes involved a lot of projects. Once again, I was learning that my way was not always the best way, and it was imperative that I trust God's leading for every area of my life. My internship interview was successful, and I was due to start after the holiday break. The extra time gave me a couple of weeks to wind down from my fall classes. I needed the time to get prepared and learn everything I possibly could about being an administrator.

Time passed very quickly, and we were in Ohio for almost eight months. The fall season in the Midwest is beautiful. The crisp fall air, hot apple cider, warm doughnuts, and the smell of pumpkin were only a few of the perks of living in this part of the United States. Terrence and I made frequent visits to the farmer's markets and the apple orchards. The fall season was over quickly, and there was suddenly an increase in brisk winds and colder temperatures. Winter was setting in sooner than expected, and the days grew shorter because of daylight savings time. That time of the year was certainly not my favorite time because of the constant gray overcasts and seemingly endless snowfalls. The one thing that I had to look forward to was the completion of my time as a student in the master's program at Marygrove. My dream of becoming a certified school administrator was coming true. My birthday came in October, and the following month, Joshua turned three years old. It was hard to believe that three years had passed since the most horrific time of my life. The Thanksgiving holiday was mostly a time of rest and rejuvenation for the family. Terrence finally got some time off because the factory shut down for the holiday. We had our Thanksgiving dinner catered, and we spent the rest of the day napping and watching movies. I was more excited about getting to spend time with Terrence than I was about eating turkey and dressing. The down time allowed us to survey how much we really missed being in each other's company. The text messages and occasional phone calls we made to one another during our breaks at work was just not the same to me. The Christmas holiday brought along the fierce winter we always knew would come but somehow was still dreading. The snow days were starting to pile up already, and amazingly enough, that was just the beginning of the winter season. We passed the time watching Netflix, playing video games, reading books, and taking naps. I had never been more grateful for warm clothes and a warm home than I was when we started to experience days of below-freezing temperatures. We were also blessed to have our utilities covered by the housing commission. There was still work to be done because my internship was due to start after the beginning of the year. I had a tough schedule because I had to rise early to pick Terrence up from the factory and go home where I would attempt to get a few hours of sleep before reporting to the high school. There were also days that I dropped Joshua off at daycare before going to school. That time of my life felt dreadful, but the drive to become a principal kept me going on the darkest of days. It always seemed like I was met with more resistance during the times I felt I was breaking through to the dawn of a new season.

The first few days of my internship were intense. I spent most of my time sitting in the principal's office asking questions and learning what her day was like at the high school level on a daily basis. Working with a high school was different because I came from an elementary school background. I'd previously taught third and fifth grades, respectively. I had very little experience working with high schools, except for the teen group at my previous church. Nevertheless, I felt my calling was to work with the older kids, and that calling propelled me to be open to learn how to be successful as a high school administrator. My mentor had an elementary school background as well, and the current year was her second year as a high school principal. I came in eager and ready to learn daily. I spent time before arriving at school each day compiling questions and suggestions for other ways for me to learn. The staff was curious and quiet at first, but they eventually started to get used to me and open up.

According to state guidelines, I had to prove competency for seven goals to be approved for my certification. My mentor and I had to come up with activities for me to participate in and lead. Coming up with these activities was difficult since I was not currently a staff member. I had moments when I was worried that things weren't going well because of my extreme exhaustion and the strain in communication between myself and my mentor. As time went on, I realized it was up to me and not anyone else to make this experience work so that I would finish and be approved for my certification. It would have been easy to give up and run elsewhere, but I would have only been faced with similar problems or a new set of problems.

To add to my feelings of being a misfit, I was a diagnosed with endometriosis. I started having problems with my menstrual cycle back in the late fall of 2013. After seeking a doctor's opinion and going through a series of tests, this was the unfortunate conclusion. The doctor decided to stop me from having periods in order to prevent the unbearable pain and heavy bleeding. I began a regiment of birth control shots, and of course, the shots had their own unpleasant side effects. Sadly enough, the bleeding did not completely stop with the medication. Sometimes, I felt as if my mood swings and fatigue were taking over me; nevertheless, I continued to press to finish my internship and to care for my family.

One day, I had an emotional meltdown in my mentor's office after she attempted to give me some directions in completing one of my projects. She allowed me some time alone to collect myself before we proceeded with the rest of the day. I explained to her what my health challenges were, and she encouraged me by sharing some of her own past experiences.

The days were long and exhausting. I would ordinarily arrive at the school between eight thirty and nine o'clock each morning. I would often leave for the day between one and two in the afternoon because I had to arrive home in time to drop Terrence off at work. The harsh

Ohio winter made having school virtually impossible between the months of January and March. I was very thankful that I had only 75 hours left to complete my internship, and there was flexibility to make up the time from the snow days. I spent a great deal of the school day in the deans' offices observing students as they came in late. I also observed the students who were often in the office because of behavioral referrals. There was never a dull moment during my internship, so all of the activities made the day more exciting and the time went by a lot quicker. I also had an opportunity to bond with a number of students, mostly freshman, because I was assisting the deans with a mentor program. We hoped the program would help improve student behavior, attendance, and academics. I assisted in monitoring the lunch periods, hall sweeps, and some meetings between my mentor and staff. Principal and assistant principal meetings were a great way for me to become acquainted with other administrators in the district and to become more knowledgeable of the dynamics and politics of the Toledo Public Schools. Before I knew it, the end had come and I was overseeing my last staff meeting and attending the final forum for completion of my hours. On my final day at Bowsher, the dean's secretary baked me a coffee cake and I shared it with the rest of the staff in the office. I said my goodbyes to the staff and students.

My mentor wrote an excellent review on my performance as a mentee, and that was it. It was finally finished, and commencement was about a month away. The graduate fair was scheduled a few weeks before graduation to give the graduates a chance to order invitations, class rings, caps and gowns, and to take senior portraits. I purchased my cap, gown, and my hood. Representatives from the alumni office and financial aid office assisted with setting up the exit interview process. The commencement ceremony was scheduled for the weekend of Mother's Day 2014. I received a clearance from my professor for my internship completion. My dream was now a reality. I was just days away from my victory walk in recognition of the completion of my degree program, and I would be certified as a K-12 administrator. Things were looking up for Terrence as well. He was contacted by a company that eventually set up a phone interview with him for a position at a factory. As he was going through that process, a pharmaceutical company contacted him for an interview as well. Terrence interviewed with the pharmaceutical company, and was offered the job. Graduation went off without a hitch, and that day was the happiest day of my life. Nowadays, my face is set forward to the future to continually walk the path God has set for me. My family and I have entered our season of recovery and restoration.

My story wasn't for the sake of receiving pity, but it was simply to release strength to you. No matter what you have faced in the past or what you're presently facing, broken lives can be mended when you give God all of the pieces.